Dedicated to all golfers
who play the game regularly
but can't understand why.

Stephen

How to play golf

29th Anniversary Edition

PRENTICE
HALL
PRESS

New York • London • Toronto • Sydney • Tokyo • Singapore

Baker
in the low 120's

Photographed by Howard Zieff

PRENTICE HALL PRESS
15 Columbus Circle
New York, NY 10023

Originally published by Prentice-Hall, Inc.

PRENTICE HALL PRESS and colophons are registered trademarks
of Simon & Schuster, Inc.

Library of Congress Catalog Card Number: 62-16893

ISBN 0-13-359068-2

Manufactured in the United States of America

30 29 28 27

CONTENTS:

CHAPTER ONE

How to Lower Your Score from 125 to 124

This book is written for the Sunday golfer who is out there trying to hit the ball on Friday afternoons, Saturdays, Sundays, Mondays, and any other day his absence from the office would not be noticed.

Contrary to popular belief — and a great deal of scientific evidence — not all golfers are neurotics. They only **appear** to be neurotics to the untrained observer of the sport who sees them for the first time on a golf course flailing oddly shaped mallets and sometimes breaking them, beating their heads with their fists, stomping the ground and sobbing bitterly. What the non-golfer does not understand is that these people are having fun.

True, some golfers take the game too seriously for their own good. By hearsay they learn that there exist players who consistently break 120. Excited by the idea, they also want to shoot a perfect golf game.

There is good news for these golfers: this book will show you how almost everybody with an exceptional sense of coordination, powerful muscular development, a natural "feel" for a flawless golf swing can, at one time or another, break 120.

Most players lose confidence in their ability much too soon. After ten or fifteen years of playing, a few hundred lessons, and a couple of thousand lost golf balls, they become distraught when their scores on an off-day pass the 140 mark.

Listen to what some of the professionals **in their own words**, have to say about the importance of confidence in golf:

Arnold Palmer, who has captured many a major championship in golf says, **"A golfer must have confidence."**

Jack Nicklaus, top money-maker in the business and an articulate teacher of the game says, **"A golfer must have confidence."**

And Lee Trevino, another well-known tour player and author of books on golf vastly more instructive than this one, says, **"A golfer must have confidence."**

So if you want to hit the ball, swing at it confidently even if you are losing your confidence because you keep missing the ball every time.

Any golfer serious enough about his game to want to break 120 must learn to stop worrying about the last ten or twenty missed strokes and learn to look ahead **positively** to more of the same.

Golfer gets ball off the tee, smiling **confidently.**

STROKE TWO:

Confident swing helps player to advance ball another fifty feet.

STROKE THREE:

Chip shot executed with **confidence,** propels golf ball back onto fairway.

STROKE FOUR:

STROKE FIVE:

Golfer now hits shot with renewed **confidence** and steers it to a mere fifteen feet from the pin!

With style that bespeaks of great **confidence,** the golfer plops ball back onto grass surface.

STROKE SIX:

Trap shot landed ball two hundred feet from green. Justifiably **confident** in his strength, player sends it back to the green.

Confidence, which comes from experience in shooting out of bunkers, aids golfer in placing ball a few feet away from hole.

STROKE TEN:

STROKE ELEVEN:

Nudging the ball in the general direction of the flag, the next putt now can be planned with **confidence.**

Firm, **confident** putt makes ball roll past the pin by only a few inches.

STROKE TWELVE:

Player's supreme **confidence** in himself enables him to sink the putt with authority just like a professional.

NEXT TEE:

Golfer is now ready to face the next hole with **confidence.**

The complex mechanism of a golf swing calls into action various parts of the human anatomy (see drawing). Though only a few seconds elapse between addressing the ball and missing it, much happens inside the body, involving muscle fibers, nerve cells and the lining of the stomach.

With the aid of his brain (1) the golfer decides to hit the ball. Message is forwarded to eyeballs (2a and 2b) which are fixed rigidly on the golf ball. Mouth (3) begins twitching. Heart (4) beat quickens and stomach (5) growlingly responds to pressure around the abdomen. Ulcer now starts forming. Blood leaves head, causing feeling of dizziness and spots before the eyes which golfer interprets as golf balls. Still, with a commendable display of will power, the player manages to lift club over his shoulder. Crackling noises emanate from wrist (6) and fingers (7) as they are made to bend. This noise is soon overpowered by a piercing cacophony originating from the general area of shoulders: bones grating against each other, muscles pulling at joints, ligaments stretched to near-breaking points.

A message is sent to the brain that the chances of golfer's hitting the ball are ever so slight. Brain classifies and releases all information (contradictory as it may be) about golf swing, accumulated there during many years of taking lessons. Confusion sets in. Knees (8 and 9) vibrate rhythmically like a pair of pneumatic drills. The club is now poised for a down-swing. With a powerful jerk it is brought down. The club head passes the approximate area of the golf ball, touching it gently on its way, while eyeballs remain riveted to the ground. There is a sharp pain in the stomach. Sweat glands work hard, throat is dry and the pulse accelerates twice its normal speed. Knees collapse completely.

After follow-through, twitching around mouth ceases. Lips, however, keep moving more vigorously than before. After repeated efforts, golfer is able to emit sound, made up in its entirety of ill-chosen words. This completes the cycle of golfer's reflex in hitting a golf ball—one of the true wonders of nature.

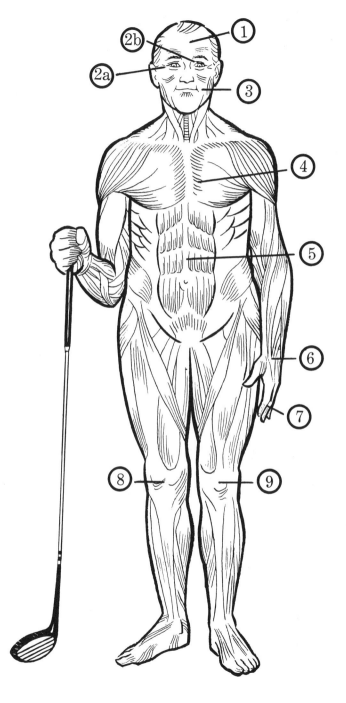

A handy list of alibis for golfers who need them

(For easy — and quick — reference, alibis here have been arranged in alphabetical order.)

Can't play on an empty stomach
Didn't get enough sleep last night
Fairways are too narrow
Grass too high in the rough
Grass too high on the fairways
Had one martini too many
Had two martinis too many
Had three martinis too many
Ha-ha-ha-had four martinis too many
Had too much to eat
I lost my job yesterday, my wife left me, the house burned down, and I feel a bit tense

I peeked
I'm about to catch a cold
It was an old ball; I don't really care*
Looked up not soon enough
Looked up too soon
Lost my grip
Lost my swing
Too early in the morning, give me time to wake up
Too late in the morning, I'm tired already
Used wrong club**
Wind shifted while ball was in the air***

*To be used when ball lands in water hazard with a splash.
**Version of this: "Caddie handed me the wrong club." You can blame almost any mishap on the caddie, provided you tip him generously enough at the end of the game.
***A favorite with the experts. Shows you are aware of the fine points of the game.

The mark of a good golfer is that he takes the divot in **front** of the ball. This shows that he was correctly hitting **down** at the ball, not trying to pick it up as so many golfers do. This golfer missed the ball the professional way.

You need golf clubs with which to hit balls, trees and the ground.

Much has been said about the proper selection of clubs. Basically, you have a choice between two kinds of sets: (1) the inexpensive or (2) the expensive. Your choice will depend on your credit rating.

Golf clubs are designed scientifically, so as to give maximum benefit to those who sell them. All golf clubs, without exception, have two ends. The part you grip is called appropriately the "grip" and the part that theoretically is supposed to come in contact with the ball is known as a "club head," a name derived from "club" and "head." These two ends of the stick are, by an ingenious arrangement, connected with a steel rod named "shaft." The shaft also serves as a means with which to hit the ball; such a stroke is usually laughingly referred to as "shanking the ball."

A professional will tell you the amount of flex you need in the shaft of your club. The more the flex, the more strength you will need to break the thing over your knees.

Clubs are made to give you as much distance as possible. Every club has its own range; no players are able to throw them away at precisely the same distance. The maximum throwing range of the club depends on the power, technique and mental state of the owner.

Here are a few examples:

	Minimum	Maximum
Driver	20 feet	50 feet
Three Wood	25 feet	60 feet
Five Iron	35 feet	70 feet
Wedge	50 feet	90 feet
Putter	75 feet	216 feet*

*This would be an unusually long throw for a golfer whose records show he could never hit the ball that far. The heave would probably have been preceded by a series of missed putts—a circumstance that might have served as an inspiration for attaining this distance.

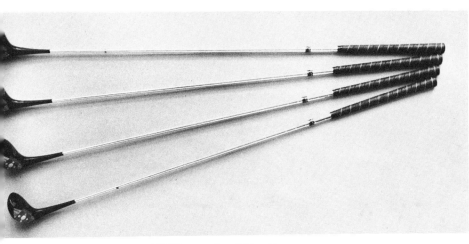

Wood Clubs

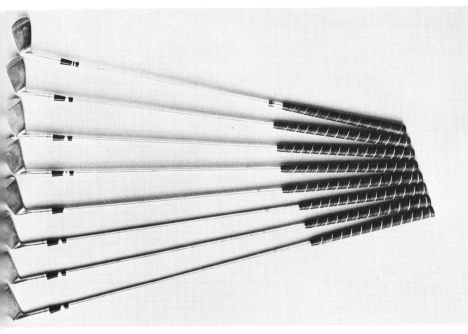

Iron Clubs

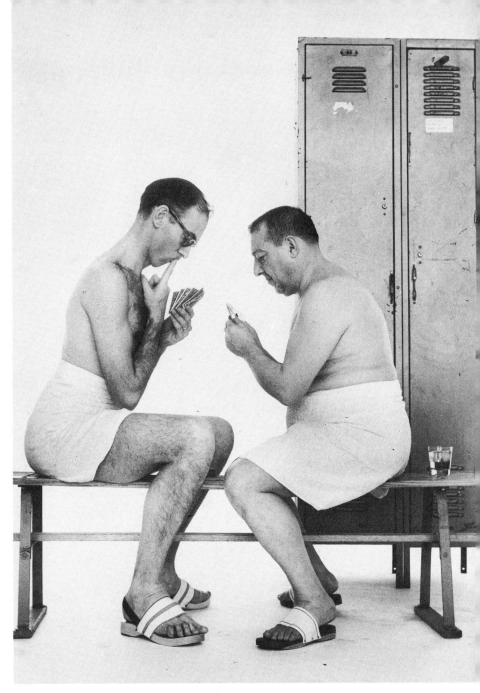

Country Clubs

Special equipment for the average golfer:

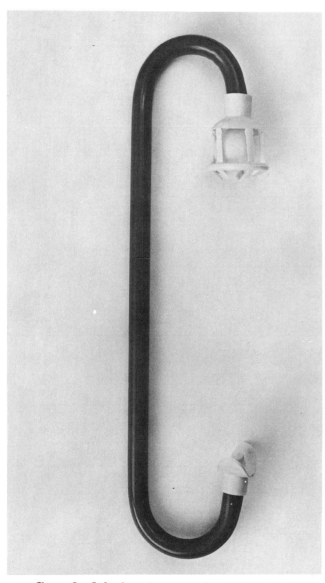

Counting machine saves time in totaling up the score.

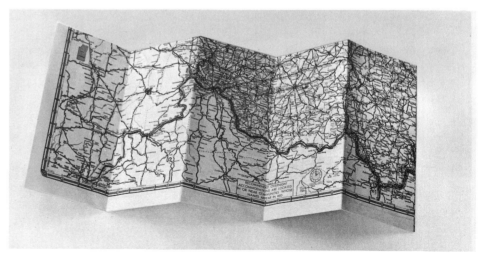

Snorkel helps in searching for ball in water hazards.

Map aids golfer looking for his ball in unknown territories.

Golf balls, a couple of dozen, keeps golfers from running out of them on eighteen holes of play.

Compass gives player a sense of direction as he tries to find his way back.

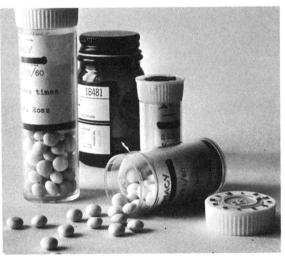

Tranquilizers make it possible for golfer to relax at his favorite form of relaxation.

Rope serves as an extra piece of equipment for those who hate to lose.

Choose headgear according to scoring ability

Average score
120

Average score
100

Average score
90

Average score
89

The manner in which you conduct yourself in a golf shop is very important. It is possible to look like an expert golfer inside a sporting goods shop even if outdoors you may be creating a different impression. Here's how:

1. **Appear casual at all times.** As you walk into the store, do not head in the general direction of the salesman. Remember, you don't really need him, you know what you want, he is there only to wrap up the clubs not to give you advice. As you walk up and down the aisles, apply the slow, deliberate walking style of professionals as they amble up to their balls lying on the fairway 250 yards off the tee. Keep your hands in your pockets and a cigarette in your mouth (if you can manage this without bursting into a coughing spell).

2. **Step up to the clubs you want.** Do not stare at them with awe. Take the cigarette out of your mouth, drop it, grind it with the heel of your shoe, and ignore the blackspot it leaves there or you may have to pay for damages. You can now begin to whistle to yourself quietly, but loud enough for the salesman (who has been watching you for some time anyway) to take notice. Reach for the club.

3. **Do not look up when the salesman approaches you.** Keep your eyes on the club. Place your forefingers on the approximate center of the shaft to check the "balance" of the club. Hold it up vertically. Throw a quick sideglance at the salesman.

4. **The salesman will ask you just what it is you want.**

5. **Tell him you have developed a slight but consistent hook in your game.** Expert golfers hook their shots. The salesman will listen to you with respect.

6. **Swing through an imaginary ball.** But be careful. Don't hit the floor, your shoes or the salesman's head. At the completion of your swing, hold your pose for a few minutes for the benefit of the audience.

7. **Pick up the box of white socks you swept off the counter as you were swinging.**

8. **The salesman will again want to know just what it is you want.**

9. **Keep him in suspense.** Expert players are cautious in their purchases. Ask him to show you some other clubs. Look at them all, the clubhead, the shaft, the grip, and hold them up against the light, squinting your eyes as you would against the sun on a golf course. Swing them wildly.

10. **Stop swinging suddenly and tell the salesman you found the club you were looking for.** Explain to him that the club has just the right whip, the right grip, the right length, the right balance, and most importantly, the right "feel."

11. **Repeat the word "feel" as often as possible.** Nobody knows just what it means. Keep talking about it as you follow the salesman to the cash register.

12. **Exit the store, with the same slow, deliberate pace you used coming in.**

CHAPTER TWO

How to Lower Your Score from 124 to 123

The gyrostatic movements the golfer goes through in order to hit the ball are referred to, not too surprisingly, as his **swing.** We say that a golfer "swings at the ball"; his hands swing, his body swings and sometimes—after he has hit the ball—his head swings gloomily back and forth, too.

A smooth, flowing swing is an asset on a golf course. Even if the golfer can't for the life of him hit that ball, he can still impress his friends and the caddie with his flawless practice swings.

A sign of a seasoned golfer is the **grooved swing.** The secret of a grooved swing is **consistency.** Hands, arms, hips move back the same way every time, and the down-swing more or less follows the same pattern (see illustration on the right) as the back-swing. As a result, the golfer misses the ball in precisely the same way every time.

There are various types of swings, depending on the size, weight, and drinking habits of the golfer. Some golfers have "bad" swings. Others, by virtue of devoted learning and tireless practicing, develop "lousy," "strange," "preposterous," "monstrous" and "utterly ridiculous" swings. There are players, especially among the elderly, having been at it for twenty or thirty years, who develop "compensatory mechanisms" to make up for the minute flaws in their swing; i.e., stamp collecting.

One of the most important ingredients of a polished swing is a **sense of timing.** Experienced golfers all admit that they possess an intuitive feel for utilizing every second. Here's how:

Start of back-swing at the first tee: 9 A.M.
Completion of swing at the last putt at the eighteenth hole: 11:30 A.M.
Arrival at the bar in the club house: 11:31 A.M.
Ordering first drink: 11:32 A.M.
Settling bets: 12:30 P.M.
Ordering third drink: 12:31 P.M.
Still trying to settle bets: 1:30 P.M.
Ordering fourth drink: 1:45 P.M.
Description of fourteenth hole to the bartender: 2:00 P.M.
Shooting dice: 2:30 P.M.
One more drink: 2:35 P.M.
Description of fourteenth hole to the bartender: 2:37 P.M.
Singing under the shower, splashing about, saying "hello" to an old acquaintance in the next shower booth: 2:45 P.M.
Looking for the locker: 2:46 P.M.
Calling locker room attendant to help find locker: 2:55 P.M.
Beginning of a three-hour poker game: 3:05 P.M.
Calling wife to explain why golf game is taking so long: 4:30 P.M.
Going to the pro shop to browse around a bit: 6:06 P.M.
Talking to the pro about the fourteenth hole: 6:22 P.M.
Purchase of a new putter: 6:23 P.M.
Purchase of a new three wood club: 6:35 P.M.
Purchase of a complete set of clubs with leather bag and a dozen golf balls at marked down prices: 7:21 P.M.
Another call to wife: 7:23 P.M.
Three more quick drinks at the bar following conversation with wife: 7:25 P.M.
Singing with friends at the bar: 7:35 P.M.
Leaving the club: 9:00 P.M.

1. Golfer tees up ball and stares at it for a few minutes. This gives him time to think about the shot he is about to make.

2. He slowly brings club back, gripping it firmly. He is experienced enough to know that without a back-swing there is no down-swing.

3. He continues to move club with deliberation while mentally checking his grip, stance, hip movement and position of his cap.

7. *@#*&@#*

8. Still keeping an eye on the ball, he lets his club travel low while right knee is beginning to buckle.

9. The club continues to move while the golfer makes a strong—but graceful—wind-up for a follow-through.

4. At the top of his back-swing, he lets the club linger for a while to gather momentum for forthcoming shot.

5. Down-swing begins. Note fluidity of head movement, shifting back and forth from original position, allowing free body action.

6. Generating tremendous power, the golfer shows a determined effort to make club head meet ball.

10. Wrists are now beginning to break as are elbows, fingers, toes.

11. His eye **still** on the ball, he now manages to completely regain his balance.

12. Perfect follow-through lends golfer an air of professional authority.

FRONT VIEW   REAR VIEW

TOP VIEW

The follow-through is the most important part of the golf swing. It is the golfer's best—and sometimes only—opportunity to **look** good on the golf course. It is the most impressive of all poses to strike up when being photographed; thus the profusion of follow-through pictures of golfers. Stay in this pose on a golf course as long as you can without holding up the foursome behind you.

Remember: at the completion of the swing, throw your club out **after the ball.**

In playing the bunker shot, pay attention to the professional's advice: **Plant your feet firmly in the sand.** (See left-hand page.)

Once buried in, wiggle your feet around. This will enable you to determine the consistency of the sand. After you have executed the shot, if ever, take your shoes and socks off and shake the grit out from between your toes.

There are as many ways to get out of traps as there are getting into them. Most golfers use the sand wedge for this shot. Others reach for the putter, especially when the bunker is shallow, and still others, when nobody is watching, scoop the ball out with the palm of their hands.
Playing out of a bunker really isn't as difficult as some golfers think. Listen to what the professionals have to say:

> Arnold Palmer says, "Playing out of a bunker is easy."
> Jack Nicklaus says, "Playing out of a bunker is easy."
> Lee Trevino says, "Playing out of a bunker is easy."

Make sure you hit **down** at the ball, about an inch behind it. This will enable the club face to dig into the sand and send forth a heavy blast of sand which will rise wearily into a familiar mushroom shape. Once the sand particles have dispersed in the air, filling up your mouth and nostrils, the ball lying in front of you, exactly in the same position, will once again be visible.

Golfer addresses ball lying in a bunker.

The follow-through.

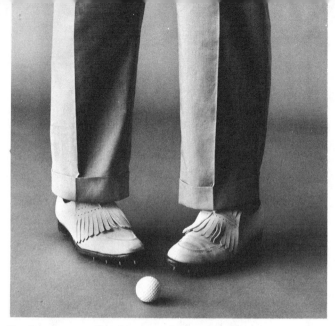

Faulty stance: Feet are too **close** together

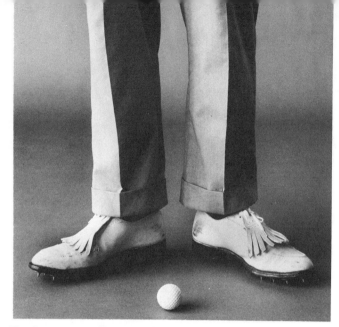

Faulty stance: Feet are too **far** apart

Faulty stance: Golfer is too **near the ball**

Faulty stance: Golfer is too **nervous**

The manner in which the golfer stands while desperately trying to hit the ball is called his **stance.**

It is important that the golfer, when taking up a position to address the ball, have his feet on the ground. Most experts agree that hitting a golf shot while floating in mid air represents a formidable task; the clubs are usually too short to reach the ball.

The average player has a tendency to fall flat on his face at the completion of the swing, or awkwardly topple sideways on the backswing. Poor balance may be the cause of all this or possibly a few drinks between rounds. A firmer stance and a little more moderation in drinking will help to correct these errors.

You can always tell a good golfer by his legwork; the way he stands up to the ball, walks, taps his feet on the ground as he waits. You can also learn much from the subtle way professionals manipulate their stances as they plan to steer the ball around obstacles, encouraging a fade or a draw. You may try to do the same; to get rid of a slice, for example, bring your left foot slightly forward. This will cut down your **slicing** the ball and make it **hook** true and far out of bounds.

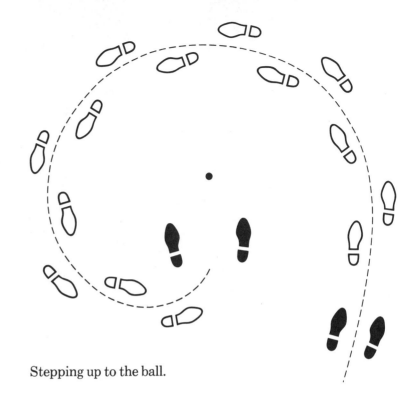

Stepping up to the ball.

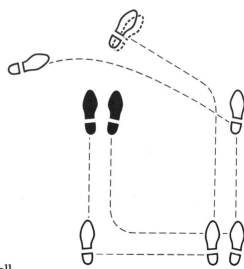

Stepping away from a well-hit ball

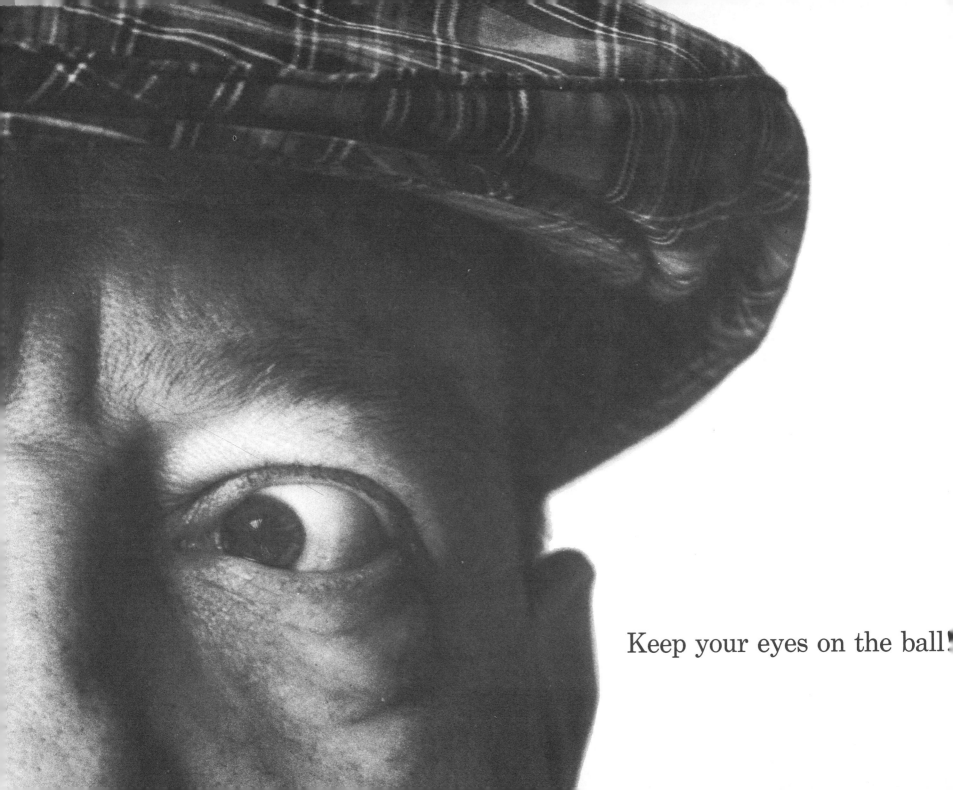

Keep your eyes on the ball!

Not all players are able to get along with their caddies, and so they spoil not only their games, but more importantly, the caddie's fun. You must always remember that the average caddie is a far better golfer than you; and therefore, by simple logic he feels **he** should be the one playing golf and you should be carrying the bag.

Some caddies are professional-golfers-to-be, using their spare time, as when walking from the green to the next tee, to work diligently on their swings. A number of well-known golfers received their early training in this way. A notable exception is Dwight Eisenhower who started his career as a military man.

Just as there are caddies who are professional-golfers-to-be, there are professional golfers who are caddies-to-be. That is the way with the world.

Caddies come in all sizes, shapes, shirts, hats, caps, trousers and underwear. You must make sure that you find a caddie with whom you will be compatible. There are many caddies at large willing to accompany you in your journey into the wilderness:

The Career Caddie keeps his feelings to himself and is surprised at nothing. He has long ceased to marvel at the folly of golfers; he expects your drive to fade, and the very instant you have completed your swing he heads right for the exact spot in the rough. He has a repertoire of soothing remarks at his disposal ("A tricky green, everybody misses it," or "The sand is wet today" or "You had the distance all right") which he utters with seeming earnestness while at the same time he sizes up your potentials as a tipper.

The Winner of the Last Caddie Tournament can't understand your reasons for being on a golf course. Though he makes a commendable effort in keeping his opinions from you, he commits himself more often than the Career Caddie. He winces perceptibly and looks away as you're swinging at the ball. Prompted for advice two hundred feet away from the green, he will readily suggest that you play for the roll on the left side of the pin. At the end of the game he is likely to offer you lessons at a reasonable rate behind the clubhouse during lunch hours.

The Talkative Type Caddie would like to turn caddying for you into a social event. He is an extrovert. Between the first and the eighteenth hole, you will get the unabridged story of his life. He claims he loves his line of work because it takes him outdoors. You learn that before he became a caddie he was an important figure in the hotel chain business, but he never did enjoy the rat race, so one day, just like that, he quit his position. He was a bus boy. He admits slyly that he used to take a drink now and then—like a few sips with his toast at breakfast, but that's all in the past now; he hasn't touched the stuff since yesterday noon. This caddie, you will soon find out, is anxious to please. He will plunge after your ball in the heaviest of foliage, and his sense of responsibility won't permit him to make a reappearance without the ball even if it takes him hours to find it.

The Businessman Caddie, it just so happens, knows of a set of clubs, practically brand new, going at a bargain rate. They belong to a friend of his who needs the money so he can offer financial aid to his grandmother who needs new tires on her 1950 Chevrolet. He admits frankly he is not qualified to give you golf lessons; but he knows of several caddies with whom he can set up an appointment for you at ridiculously low prices. He has an uncanny ability for finding golf balls, usually while he is searching for yours. These he passes on to various members of his business combine located at strategic points adjacent to the fairways. In the dusk, after the sun and golfers have had their day, you will find him with his smiling countenance floating freely on the surface of the largest body of water on the course. While in the murky depths his prehensile toes are hard at work in quest of golf balls. He is a dependable source of short term loans to his dice-throwing colleagues; his rate of interest is low, or so it seems to him. This type of caddie you may meet again next year— as a member of the club.

The Pessimist Caddie likes to take a realistic view of the situation. "I don't think you'll make it over the water, sir," he will say, and surprisingly enough, things turn out just as predicted. "This will be a difficult hole, sir," he will warn you, and again he astounds you with his keen foresight. It is his opinion that you tend to underclub yourself. He encourages you to hit a provisional ball off the tee since the chances of finding your first ball are ever so slight. Following his suggestion, you do hit another ball, only to learn that now you have lost not one, but **two** balls.

The Youngest Caddie of All measures less than five feet in height, weighs about 110 pounds, and wants very much to work. At the fifth hole you notice his knees tremble frightfully. Calling the expedition to a temporary halt, you suggest he should rest. At the seventh hole, you take one bag away from him, on the eleventh you insist he hand over the other bag. On the fifteenth hole you put your arms around him to help keep him in an upright position. On the seventeenth you pick him up and tote him back to the club house.

Caddie handing over the club

Golfer takes a few practice swings

Golfer hits the ball

Caddie taking back the club

CHAPTER THREE

How to Lower Your Score from 123 to 122

This chapter is about **problem** shots in golf.

All problem shots have one thing in common: they represent a problem to the golfer. A surprisingly large percentage of golf shots belong in this category. More specifically, **all** shots in golf are problem shots, except possibly that shot of whisky you, as if by magic, make disappear with a single gulp on the nineteenth hole.

It may be comforting to know that even professionals have problem shots. A top golfer, for example, having won an important tournament, was overheard complaining that he thought it was most difficult to make an eagle on one of the long par five holes.

Remember, it isn't always your fault that you are faced with the problem of completing a shot. The mistake was made originally by the architect commissioned to lay out the course. Golf architects are a notoriously mean lot who work out their unconscious hostilities toward their fellow beings by designing fairways and greens.

For example, they make fairways too narrow, bunkers too deep, putting surfaces too far from the greens. They talk about placing hazards at the "most strategic locations" on the course, but all that talk is only a cover-up for poor planning. After all, everyone knows that water holes, sand traps, trees and other such obstacles only get in the way and unnecessarily complicate the rounds of a golfer.

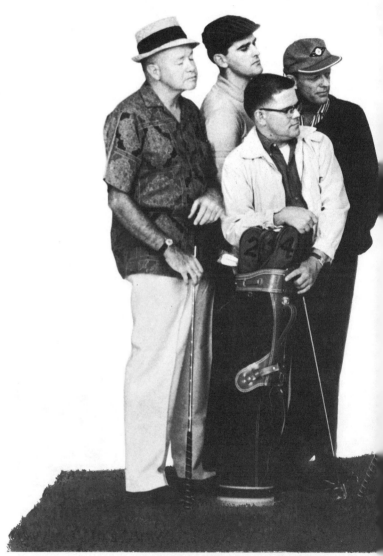

Problem Shot No. 1: The first tee

Problem Shot No. 2: Water hazard

Problem Shot No. 3: Approaching the green from the adjoining fairway

Problem Shot No. 4: Uphill lie

Problem Shot No. 5: Downhill lie (the opposite of uphill lie)

Problem Shot No. 6: Hitting off from top of a tree

Problem Shot No. 7: Getting the ball away from a tree

Problem Shot No. 8: Ball resting on a highway in midst of heavy traffic

Problem Shot No. 9: The nineteenth hole

Plan: Drive to land right side of fairway, safe distance from trap. Next ball to plop on green, followed by two putts.

Plan: Aim tee shot at front of bunker. Then onto the green. Add two putts.

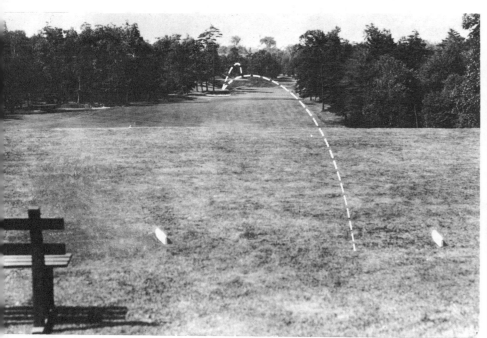

Plan: Powerful drive carries the ball behind the trap, then comes a short chip. Two putts make for par.

Plan: Conservative drive down the center, makes approach to the green simple. Two putts complete the hole.

Execution of plan as demonstrated in this photograph points out minute differences between the way golfer intended to play hole and the way he actually played it. Apparently he did not take into consideration all factors; i.e., direction of wind, grain of grass, angle of slopes.

It isn't too hard to learn how to contemplate. You can get some practice right in front of the mirror in your own home. Knit your eyebrows and master the skill of raising and lowering them. Work out a technique of **thoughtfully** lighting a cigarette. Learn to blow the smoke out against the wind without choking. Before you swing at the ball, take the caddie into your confidence and discuss with him the various possibilities. This will impress your partners, if not the caddie.

Shown to the right are three kinds of tee shots, all popular with the average golfer. The **chip drive** (1) sends the ball up to impressive heights (a 200-yard drive is not unheard of: 100 yards up and 100 yards down), provided you are a powerful hitter. The **pitch drive** (2) bounces for several yards if the ground is hard. **Putt drive** (3) is effective when playing against strong wind. In this shot the ball rolls on the ground and comes to a slow halt not very far from the tee.

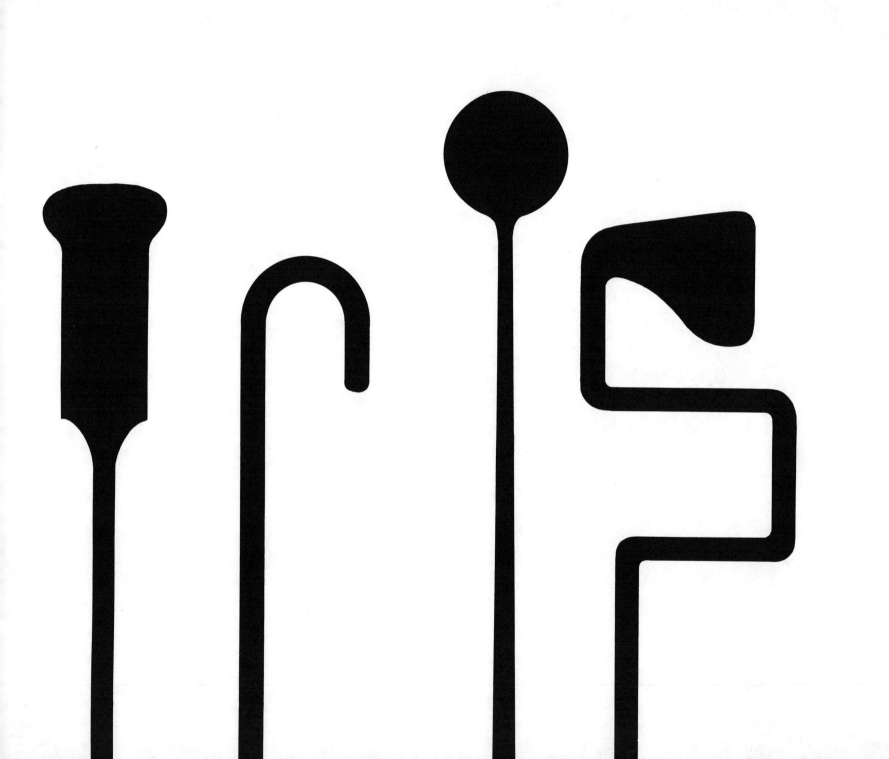

Find a putter which suits your personality.
Putters, just as the people who use them, come in
a variety of types. No matter what your approach
to putting, remember there is always a putter
available to you for the asking, provided you
have the money.

In order to break 121 or even 122 you must
learn the secret of putting. Many golfers miss
their chances for low scores on the greens.
They get there in six or seven expertly played
shots but then waste three or four strokes trying
to sink the ball. Simple arithmetic shows that
four putts on every hole make a total of
seventy-two strokes. This is a nice round figure
but presents the golfer who wants to par the
course with a serious problem.

People often wonder about the size of the cup
on the green. By official dictum the diameter of
this depression must be four and a quarter inches,
no more and no less. It is easy to understand
how this size has been arrived at. If the hole
were smaller or larger, the flagstick would simply
not fit.

Learn to read the green

●

Remember: The hole is only as big as it looks to you!

Concentrate. Don't let the watching eyes of a few spectators disturb you!

Once you have started the ball rolling in the approximate direction of the hole, you can begin refining your follow-through technique.

Though no two golfers have exactly the same putting style in following through, the fundamental concept remains the same.
For reminders, here are some do's and don'ts:

Do twist your body in the shape of a pretzel as you try to coax the ball.

Do stand on your toes, then fall into a slouch.

Do revolve around your axis a few times while the ball moves toward the cup.

Do talk to the ball.

Don't burst into tears.

Don't hit your caddie.

Don't lose your balance while you are jumping up and down.

Don't dive into the nearest sand trap just because the ball did not drop into the cup.

HOW TO "TALK" GOLF

Anybody can learn to **talk** golf. All that is needed is a less-than-average vocabulary, acting ability and people who are willing to listen.

An accomplished golf-talker never relates his experiences on the course where his actions may cast some doubts on his words. He stays away from fairways and greens, the farther the better, and confines his speech making to locker rooms, business offices and living quarters.

He picks his audience with care. Rarely does he waste his talents on expert golfers who may think that physical exercise is more important than mental exercise. Rather, he concentrates on those who are interested in the finer things in life, such as talking.

Golf should never be talked about in a sitting position. The lecturer, in order to gain maximum effectiveness, should **act out** his stories. He should take imaginary swings at imaginary balls, using as wide an arc as there is room, holding the follow-through position for several minutes for everyone to see. Squinted eyes, focused at the imaginary ball taking off into space are an essential. If attention is waning, the speaker may even want to stand up on the chair, and tower over his listeners. For reasons of safety, however, he should take only short back swings at the imaginary ball.

Regardless of his score, an experienced golf-talker can always impress his audience with the virtuosity of his playing. A few simple rules may help you in achieving the desired effect:

1. Blame your high score on missed putts. Say: "This wasn't my day for putting," or: "Those three-putt greens are killing my score."

2. Talk about the way you played the hole a day before, last week, last year or when you were still young. Nobody will remember anyway.

3. Tell them this is only your first year of playing golf. If someone, by chance, recalls your presence on the course as far back as fifteen years ago, admit it but explain that you put away your clubs for fourteen years and just took them from the attic to start playing again. Say you have been at it **"on and off."**

4. Describe **in detail** the complexity of bets you made with your partners. The more confusing, the better. Talk expertly about Nassaus with Press Bets with bonuses for Birdies and Eagles and Bobs and Greenies, Low Ball Low Totals which you have combined with syndicate betting. Your audience will listen with mixed feelings of respect and boredom and you will be able to draw their attention away from your total net score.

5. Learn to use correct terminology. In golf, no matter how poorly you play, there is an explanation for everything. Examples are shown on the opposite page.

DON'T SAY:	SAY:
"I got out of a sand trap"	"I blasted out of a sand trap"
"I drove the ball into the rough"	"I hooked the ball into the rough"
"My partner outdrove me"	"I used psychology"
"Sliced my drive"	"I was playing for position to get a shot at the green but miscalculated"
"Didn't get any distance on my drive"	"Decided to play for accuracy"
"Missed the putt"	"Read the green wrong"
"Didn't reach the green on that par three hole"	"I underclubbed myself"
"Ball rolled over the green"	"Didn't put an underspin on it"
"Didn't make it over the water hazard"	"Played it safe"
"Played to the left but missed and the ball hit a tree"	"I was trying to get over the tree but didn't make it"
"Came in with a lousy score"	"My team lost money today"

CHAPTER FOUR

How to Lower Your Score from 122 to 121

Time will come when you as a so-called golfer will **know** what makes a good swing. You will now understand why it is practically impossible for you to hit the ball.

A golf swing seems simple only to the novice who doesn't know the first thing about it. As you learn the fine points of the game, and spend all the lunch allowance your wife gives you on books which analyze the golf swing so even you can understand, you will find out that there is more to it than simply hitting the ball straight down the fairway 250 feet every time. You will learn the ingredients of a perfect golf swing. Once you have acquired this intelligence you will begin missing the ball consistently, but you will be so much more able to explain to everyone's benefit what you have done wrong.

The main thing is to practice, practice and practice. Take your clubs with you wherever you go; to the office, to restaurants, to the theatre. If flourishing the clubs annoys those you hit over the head, and you carry no insurance, then dispose of the clubs and use only your arms.

Keep swinging those arms of yours while you amble down the street, or ride on a crowded elevator, or stand before the magistrate's court charged with making a public nuisance of yourself.

The best place to refine your swing is, of course, right out on the practice range. Here you will be able to watch others who have similar swings to yours. You will have an opportunity to make the same mistakes over and over again so that you no longer have to think about them, and they become part of your game.

The best time to visit the driving range is at night when you can hardly see the ball. As the little white spot soars into the distance of a few yards, it will disappear into the darkness and you will be able to imagine that you have just hit another one of your mighty drives into the evening breeze.

If you don't succeed at first, don't despair. Remember, it takes time to learn to play golf; most players spend their entire life time finding out about the game before they give up.

It is easy to develop a good golf swing once you have learned to remember a few simple pointers:

Keep your eyes on the ball

Don't stare at the ball

Don't move your head

Don't break your wrists too early at the back-swing

Relax. Tension will ruin your swing

Don't let hands and shoulders initiate the movement from the top of back-swing

Whip your right hand into the shot at the last minute to get maximum distance

Don't hurry your swing

Don't bring your club back too far   Don't sway your body

To get maximum power, accelerate the speed of your club

Hit with your hands

Forget about arms, shoulders, hips. Concentrate on cocking the wrists

Keep your wrists flexible

Take a full swing

Right-hand grip should be relaxed   Turn your hips

Club and hands should move as a single unit

Bend your knees slightly

Right knee breaks toward the left knee

Take the club back low along the ground

Hit down at the ball

Weight shifts back to the right leg

Keep your feet firmly on the ground

Don't stand too far from the ball

Hit through the ball

Don't hit from the outside in

Hit the ball if possible

Concentrate   Synchronize your movements

Don't think about your swing. Let your muscles do the work

Body action will give you power

Source of power is your left hand

Forget about hips, wrists, arms. Concentrate on turning the shoulders

Left arm should not be too stiff

Grip the club tightly   Back is straight

Left arm should be straight

Forget about shoulders, hips, wrists. Concentrate on keeping the left arm straight

Try to get hands slightly in front of the club head

Hips and shoulders should be coiling

There should be a slight lateral move in your hips

Don't delay wrist action   Bend forward slightly

Forget about arms, shoulders, wrists. Concentrate on hip movement

Get your grip right, and all other progress follows

Don't let your knees buckle

No two golfers have the same swing. Adjust yours to your physical qualifications

All golfers have the same basic swing

Hit in front of the ball

Put your weight back on your heels

Left ankle is rolled slightly toward the right foot

Don't stand too close to the ball

Lift your left heel off the ground

Don't hit from the inside out

How to shoot a birdie:

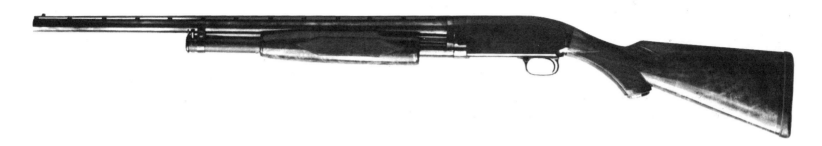

Winchester Trap Gun

Capacity: 7—2¾" Super Seal Crimp shells; magazine holds 6 (Factory installed removable plug limits magazine capacity to 2). Barrel: New Winchester Ventilated Rib. 30" full choke, 12 gauge only. Overall length: 49¾". Weight: 8¼ lbs.

Francotte

Supplied in 12, 16, 20 and 28 gauge with 2¾" chambers; .410 gauge with 3" chambers. Siemens-Martin fluid steel barrels in 6" to 30" lengths, any borings from full choke to cylinder. Automatic ejectors, straight, half or full pistol grip, selected walnut stock, horn butt plate. Weight: 13 lbs.

You must never forget that golf is supposed to be a game of relaxation. It should take your mind off your work, your mortgage, your income tax, and introduce fresh and much more serious problems into your life. An unhappy golfer is never a happy golfer, everybody knows that.

You must make every effort to relax at golf or else you will keep missing the ball which will make it impossible for you to relax. Admittedly, it isn't easy to relax; it's a considerable strain on the nervous sytem.

Give vent to your temper once in a while so that you don't go completely beserk at the end of the game. Furious as you may be, however, always act like a gentleman. If you must stomp on the fairway, replace the turf. If you must shout at your caddie for handing you a club which, in your opinion, was the sole reason for your missing the ball, tip him generously to regain his friendship. Don't ever hit anybody even in the wildest of rage; it is not only against the law, but more importantly he may hit you in return, and then what do you do?

Five ways to work off your ill temper are demonstrated on the next few pages.

Smoke a few cigarettes between rounds

Strike up a spirited conversation with your partners

Whistle

Beat the ground with your fists

Break your clubs

Stand on your head

The question often has
been asked: What is the
best way to relax between
rounds?

After much research,
golfers may be happy to
learn, it was possible to
find not one, but **ten**
solutions to the problem.
Here they are: (as shown
on these pages)

1. Martini
2. Whisky Sour
3. Scotch on the rocks
4. Old Fashioned
5. Manhattan
6. Bloody Mary
7. Tom Collins
8. Gin and Tonic
9. Beer
10. Alka Seltzer

After a few drinks, appearance of fairway improves with golfer's mental outlook;

he now misses his shots with a hearty chuckle.

Eventually all golfers suffer a nervous collapse.

This is to be expected. Golf, after all, makes tremendous demands on the golfer, frustrating him constantly, often driving him into moods of depression. Not every individual reacts to the insistent pressure of playing golf exactly the same way, depending on his personality, family background, and early toilet training. But sooner or later everyone gives in under the strain.

It is easy to recognize the symptoms:

1. The golfer can no longer function in his job, and he is about to lose it.

2. His wife and children no longer recognize him when and if he comes home.

3. He suffers from acute indigestion, insomnia, heart palpitations, high blood pressure, dizzy spells, a nervous facial tic, stutter.

4. He talks in his sleep about golf shots he should have made.

5. His doctor insists that he stop driving himself, find ways to take time off from his golf; perhaps develop a hobby.

It is advisable at this point to try to kick the golf habit for a few days and think the situation over. The expert advice of those versed in emotional problems, such as psychiatrist or priest, may be helpful.

The analysis, of course, may take months, or perhaps years, before the patient can be declared cured. But usually the treatment proves to be a success. One golfer, for example, after visiting his analyst for over a year because of consistent slicing in his drives and the resultant emotional turmoil suffered, was sent home completely freed from his problem. He was told his back-swing was too fast.

The reader, having gone through this book, may wonder at this point if it is really worth playing golf at all. He should be quickly told that most certainly golf is a worthwhile pastime. While it may make demands on the player's energy, it is a game that takes him **outdoors.** It provides him with the much-needed opportunity to **come in contact with nature**: enjoy the ozone-filled air, the gentle splash of water, the crunch of fallen leaves under thickly foliaged trees....

CHAPTER FIVE

What You Should Do When You've Scored 120

QUIT WHILE YOU'RE AHEAD!

Author STEPHEN BAKER has designed
and written over a dozen books on subjects
that range from sublime to ridiculous. His
HOW TO LIVE WITH A NEUROTIC DOG
and the hardcover version of HOW TO PLAY
GOLF IN THE LOW 120's both have been
longtime best sellers. A well-known art direc-
tor and writer, he has garnered over 60 awards
for creative excellence; his "Let Your Fingers
Do The Walking" is one of the most durable
slogans in America. He lives in East Side
Manhattan with his family and model/beauty-
expert wife Oleda, herself an author of over
ten books. Here, he says, "he practices his golf
assiduously, taking divots from the living
room carpet *in front of the ball* as good golfers
are supposed to do".

Photographer HOWARD ZIEFF launched
his career in New York as a still-life photographer, quickly rising to fame for his warm,
humorous approach to "people pictures." His
television commercials for Alka Seltzer,
Volkswagen, Volvo and many other adver-
tisers were heralded as breakthroughs in the
field. He finally succumbed to the call of
Hollywood, where he has directed such major
films as *Slither*, *Housecall*, and *The Main
Event* among others. He loves his work even
though he admits that it has interfered with
his golf on a number of occasions.

CREDITS

Outdoor table, chairs: John B. Salterini Co., Inc.

Adding Machine: Ideal Business Machines, Inc.

Winchester and Francotte Guns:
Abercrombie & Fitch

Model's name: Frank Bianco (who is not
the duffer he appears to be)

Also: United States Golf Association for
their kind permission to use several
photographs in this book.